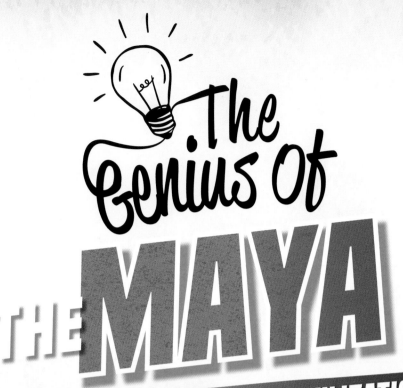

The Genius Of
THE MAYA
INNOVATIONS FROM PAST CIVILIZATIONS

IZZI HOWELL

CRABTREE
PUBLISHING COMPANY
WWW.CRABTREEBOOKS.COM

CRABTREE
PUBLISHING COMPANY
WWW.CRABTREEBOOKS.COM

Published in Canada
Crabtree Publishing
616 Welland Avenue
St. Catharines, ON
L2M 5V6

Published in the United States
Crabtree Publishing
PMB 59051
350 Fifth Ave, 59th Floor
New York, NY 10118

Published in 2020 by Crabtree Publishing Company

First published in Great Britain in 2019 by The Watts Publishing Group
Copyright © The Watts Publishing Group 2019

Author: Izzi Howell

Editorial director: Kathy Middleton

Editors: Izzi Howell, Petrice Custance

Proofreader: Melissa Boyce

Series designer: Rocket Design (East Anglia) Ltd

Designer: Steve Mead

Prepress technician: Tammy McGarr

Print coordinator: Katherine Berti

Consultant: Philip Parker

The website addresses (URLs) included in this book were valid at the time of going to press. However, it is possible that contents or addresses may have changed since the publication of this book. No responsibility for any such changes can be accepted by either the author or the Publisher.

Printed in the U.S.A./072019/CG20190501

Photo credits:
Alamy: Chico Sanchez 9b, Diego Grandi 26; Getty: SimonDannhauer title page and 13t, Rainer Soegtrop 5t, Ronaldo Schemidt/AFP 7t, Werner Forman/Universal Images Group 9t, 23b and 24, jeffwqc 11b, Dorling Kindersley 15t, cinoby 15b, Photos.com 17t, PicturePartners 19t, lucagal 20b, DEA / G. DAGLI ORTI 22, diegograndi 25t, XiFotos 28; LACMA: Purchased with funds provided by Camilla Chandler Frost 3t, 27t, 27c and 27b, The Phil Berg Collection 29br; The Metropolitan Museum: Gift of Charles and Valerie Diker, 1999 6, Gift of Arthur M. Bullowa, 1989 29t, The Michael C. Rockefeller Memorial Collection, Bequest of Nelson A. Rockefeller, 1979 29bl; Shutterstock: Tono Balaguer cover, Diego Grandi 5b, Vaclav Sebek 8, Kamira 10, Leon Rafael 11t, Madrugada Verde 12–13b and 30–31, PRILL 14l, Matyas Rehak 14r, Peter Hermes Furian 17b, Kevin Wells Photography 18, matkub2499 19cl, timquo 19cr, muratart 20t, Alexander Sviridov 21, Songchai W 23t, soft_light 25b; Stefan Chabluk 4; Wikimedia: Goran tek-en 16t; Yale University Art Gallery 3b, 7bl, 7br, 16b and 19b.

All design elements from Shutterstock.

Every attempt has been made to clear copyright. Should there be any inadvertent omission please apply to the publisher for rectification.

Library and Archives Canada Cataloguing in Publication

Title: The genius of the Maya / Izzi Howell.
Names: Howell, Izzi, author.
Series: Genius of the ancients.
Description: Series statement: The genius of the ancients | Includes index.
Identifiers: Canadiana (print) 20190108444 |
   Canadiana (ebook) 20190108460 |
   ISBN 9780778765752 (hardcover) |
   ISBN 9780778765950 (softcover) |
   ISBN 9781427123923 (HTML)
Subjects: LCSH: Mayas—Juvenile literature. | LCSH: Mayas—Antiquities—Juvenile literature. | LCSH: Technological innovations—Central America—Juvenile literature. | LCSH: Technological innovations—Mexico—Juvenile literature. | LCSH: Civilization, Ancient—Juvenile literature.
Classification: LCC F1435 .H69 2019 | DDC j972.81/016—dc23

Library of Congress Cataloging-in-Publication Data

Names: Howell, Izzi, author.
Title: The genius of the Maya / Izzi Howell.
Description: New York, New York : Crabtree Publishing Company, 2020. | Series: The genius of the ancients | Audience: Ages: 9-12. | Audience: Grades: 4-6. | Includes index.
Identifiers: LCCN 2019014239 |
   ISBN 9780778765752 (hardcover) |
   ISBN 9780778765950 (pbk.) |
   ISBN 9781427123923 (Electronic)
Subjects: LCSH: Mayas--Juvenile literature. | Mayas--Antiquities--Juvenile literature. | Technological innovations--Central America--Juvenile literature. | Technological innovations--Mexico--Juvenile literature. | Civilization, Ancient--Juvenile literature.
Classification: LCC F1435 .H83 2020 | DDC 972.81--dc23
LC record available at https://lccn.loc.gov/2019014239

CONTENTS

THE MAYA

Who?

The Maya were a large group of people who lived in southern Mexico and Central America for approximately one thousand years. The Maya **civilization** reached its height between 250 C.E. and 900 C.E., during a time in history known as the Classic Period. The Maya territory was divided into **city-states** that each had their own ruler. However, people in all the city-states shared a common language, **culture**, and religion.

This map shows the location of some of the most important Maya cities across southern Mexico and Central America.

What happened?

Around 900, the Maya civilization began to decline in many southern areas. Experts aren't sure why, but it may have been due to crop failure, loss of **fertile** land, or disease. In the 1500s, Spanish invaders took over Central America and destroyed most aspects of Maya life. However, Maya culture survives today in a few areas, and approximately 6 million people still speak Mayan languages.

This statue, made in 732, is located in Copán, Honduras. It shows a Maya ruler named Waxaklajuun Ub'aah K'awiil.

The stunning **architecture** of the Maya city of Palenque can still be seen today.

KINGS AND SOCIETY

Each Maya city-state was ruled over by a king. Maya kings were considered to be all-powerful and were believed to be the connection between ordinary people and the gods.

Role of a ruler

Maya rulers inherited their role through their family. The role of a king was to rule the city-state, making decisions about trade and war and welcoming important visitors from other areas. They also took part in religious ceremonies and **rituals**. In these ceremonies and rituals, the Maya believed that the king communicated with the gods on their behalf.

WOW!

Queens occasionally ruled Maya city-states. If there was no male **heir**, a female member of the royal family ruled as queen, or, if she had a son, as **regent**, until he was old enough to take over.

This section of a Maya pot is decorated with an image of a king meeting two visitors. The visitors have brought gifts of fruit.

Names and dates

From records kept by the Maya, we know the names and dates of many rulers. They carved important information on stones and wrote it in books called **codices**. One of the most famous Maya kings was Pakal the Great. He ruled the city-state of Palenque from 615 to 683. Pakal ordered the construction of many grand buildings in the city, the remains of which can still be seen today.

Maya hierarchy

Maya society was a **hierarchy** based on importance. The king was at the top, followed by the royal family, members of the **elite**, and the rest of society.

Pakal the Great was buried wearing a mask and jewelry made from jade. Pakal's tomb was discovered in 1952, in a temple in Palenque.

This statue shows a member of the elite, dressed in his finest jewelry. Members of the elite were born into **noble** families and often worked alongside the king.

In this statue, a warrior wears a snake around his neck to **symbolize** strength.

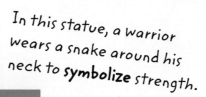

king

royal family

the elite

scribes, merchants, generals, and priests

craftspeople and warriors

farmers and laborers

enslaved people and prisoners of war

TRADE

Everyday items, such as crops, were traded by the Maya over short distances and sold to ordinary people in markets. Luxury goods, such as colored shells, were traded across long distances and sold directly to members of the elite.

Trading territories

Trade gave Maya city-states access to **natural resources** that were not available nearby. The land of the different Maya city-states was quite **diverse**. Animal skins and quetzal feathers (see right) came from the **rain forests**, jade and obsidian (see page 11) were mined in the mountains, and limestone rock was taken from low, flat lands. Salt, shells, and fish were gathered along the coast. Some city-states also traded crafted objects, such as pottery.

The feathers of the quetzal bird were luxury traded items. They were used to make headdresses worn by kings and the elite.

Peace and war

In times of peace, city-states traded natural resources fairly. However, during times of war, the winning city-state sometimes forced the losing side to hand over certain natural resources for free. As the population of some city-states grew, farmers couldn't produce enough food locally. **Importing** food from other areas was the only way to feed the population.

WOW!

The Maya did not pay for goods with coins. Basic items were exchanged. Particularly valuable items were paid for with cacao beans or precious stones, such as jade.

This Maya pottery container shows a servant (left) presenting goods to a member of the elite. The elite controlled luxury trade. Some were merchants, visiting other city-states to trade.

On the move

The Maya did not develop wheeled vehicles to transport goods. Instead, humans carried items on their backs. Traders traveled between city-states along trade routes. The trade routes had raised paved roads called *sacbeob*. Some traders traveled by water in canoes.

In some areas of Mexico and Central America, the remains of *sacbeob* can still be seen today. This one is located in Calakmul, Mexico.

9

WARFARE

Maya city-states were constantly at war with each other. For the Maya civilization, battles and violence were a normal part of everyday life.

GENIUS
ATTACK AND DEFENSE

Why war?

City-states attacked each other to show their strength and power. They also invaded other city-states to gain access to valuable trade routes and natural resources, as well as to conquer fertile farming land. Maya city-states often captured prisoners of war from conquered areas. The Maya usually killed the prisoners as **sacrifices** because they believed it pleased the gods.

This stone carving shows King Bird Jaguar IV from the city-state of Yaxchilan with a prisoner of war.

Soldiers and weapons

Maya armies were made up of ordinary men, led by kings and members of the elite. They mostly fought at close range, using weapons such as clubs, knives, and daggers. Sometimes they attacked from a distance with spears and bows and arrows.

Defense

Some Maya cities built defensive walls to protect themselves from attack. The walls enclosed the most important buildings, such as palaces and temples. The walls had an earth or stone base with wooden posts. Sometimes walls were constructed quickly to protect people from a coming attack. For example, historians believe the residents of Chunchucmil **hastily** built a wall using stones from buildings in the city center. However, it is believed the wall did not stop the invaders.

This copy of a Maya painted mural shows a winning army after battle. The soldiers are carrying spears and are wearing jaguar skins as a symbol of power and victory.

This arrowhead is made from obsidian.

(((BRAIN WAVE)))

The Maya did not develop the technology to make metal-cutting tools or weapons. However, they did create arrowheads and daggers from **flint** and obsidian, which is a hard, volcanic glass. Maya flint and obsidian blades were incredibly sharp and always cut accurately.

CITIES

Each Maya city-state was based around a city. All Maya cities were different, but most had some features in common.

GENIUS ★
THRIVING CITY CENTERS

Land and population

Maya cities were built to suit their particular **landscape** as well as the needs of the population. In hilly areas, buildings in the city center were constructed on raised areas, rather than the typical arrangement in a flat, open **plaza**. More houses were built on the city's outskirts as the population grew.

The plaza in the Maya city of Tikal in Guatemala contains two pyramids and a large palace.

In the city

The most important buildings were always built in the city center. These buildings were usually grouped together in a large central plaza. Housing was built outside of the city center. Members of the elite lived close to the center, while ordinary people lived on the outskirts.

Pyramids and palaces

The plaza of a Maya city contained important government and religious buildings, such as pyramid temples and ball courts (see pages 24 and 25). It was also home to the king, the royal family, and nobles, who lived in large palaces.

Only 10 percent of the ruins of the city of Palenque in Mexico have been uncovered. The city was abandoned sometime after 800, and was covered by growth from the rain forest.

WOW!

Researchers are using lasers to scan the rain forests, looking for hidden Maya cities and buildings. In 2018, laser scans revealed the hidden remains of 60,000 buildings in just one area!

BUILDINGS

GENIUS
★ CAREFUL CONSTRUCTION ★

A great deal of planning went into the construction of important Maya buildings. Architects paid huge attention to detail, from the shape of a building to its decoration.

Stone construction

The important buildings in the city center and homes of the elite were made from stone. Different stones were used across the city-states, depending on what was available locally. These stones included limestone, sandstone, and volcanic rocks. **Plaster** was used as cement to stick the stones together. Finally, the buildings were decorated with carvings.

Stone carvings decorate a palace in the city of Uxmal.

This is a reconstruction of the home of an ordinary Maya family. In contrast to the important city-center buildings, these houses were made from wood and dried mud, with **thatched** roofs.

Bright colors

The Maya painted the stone carvings on pyramids and palaces in bright colors. The insides of some of these buildings were also decorated with colorful painted murals.

Astronomical architecture

The shapes of some Maya buildings were inspired by **astronomy**. For example, the structure of the El Castillo pyramid at Chichén Itzá is based on Earth's orbit of the Sun. On each of the pyramid's four sides is a central panel with 91 steps. If you add up the steps on each side, plus the platform at the top, it equals 365, which is the number of days it takes Earth to orbit the Sun.

This drawing shows how a Maya pyramid would have looked after construction. Over time, almost all of the brightly painted details have worn away.

The El Castillo pyramid was a temple dedicated to Kukulkan, a Maya god that took the form of a feathered snake. The Maya worshiped many gods, some of which could take animal and human shapes.

91 steps

WRITING

The Maya had a complex writing system using symbols known as **glyphs**. They also developed their own number system, which used different shapes to represent numbers.

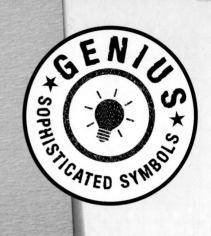

GENIUS
★SOPHISTICATED SYMBOLS★

Different glyphs

The Maya used around 800 different glyphs. Each glyph represented a word or a sound. It was the most complete writing system used in ancient Central America and Mexico.

Some words could be written using glyphs in different ways. For example, the glyph on the left represents the word jaguar, while the glyphs on the right spell out the sounds of the Mayan word for jaguar—B'alam.

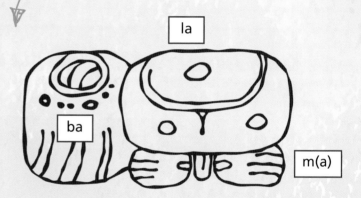

la

ba

m(a)

Creating codices

Professional scribes wrote down details of religious ceremonies and kept astronomical records in codices. The pages of codices were made from soft bark. The pages were folded like a fan to create a book.

Scribes used thin brushes to paint glyphs onto codices. In this image painted on a Maya pottery container, a scribe is holding a paint pot in his hands, with rolled bark pages under his arm.

TEST OF TIME

Spanish invaders destroyed Maya codices whenever they found them. In doing so, they erased huge quantities of ancient knowledge and records. Only four Maya codices survived. The Spanish did not allow the Maya to continue writing in their language, but it survived orally. Today, Mayan is spoken by 6 million people.

This is a page from the Dresden Codex, one of only four Maya codices that survive today.

Counting

In the Maya number system, a shell shape represented zero, a dot represented one, and a line represented five. The Maya number system was base 20, or they counted by 20s. The system we use today is base 10. The Maya are believed to be one of the first cultures to recognize the importance of representing zero.

Adding and subtracting most numbers from 1–19 is very simple with Maya numerals. Simply combine the symbols to create the answer!

17

FARMING AND FOOD

The Maya developed farming and **irrigation** techniques that allowed them to grow food in different areas. They also fished and hunted animals, such as deer.

Fertilizing farmland

It is hard to grow crops in rain forests, as the soil there isn't very fertile. The Maya made the rainforest soil fertile through a slash-and-burn process. They cut down and burned wild plants. The ash left the soil fertile enough that the Maya could grow crops there for several years. After that, they had to clear and plant in a new area.

Some people living in the Central American rain forest still practice slash-and-burn farming on a small scale.

(((BRAIN WAVE)))

Some areas in Maya city-states had almost no freshwater in the ground. The Maya carved well-like chambers called *chultuns* into the rock. These chambers filled with water when it rained. Villagers could use this water during periods of drought. It is believed some *chultuns* were used for food storage, and possibly even human burials.

Key crops

The key foods in the Maya diet were corn, beans, and squash. The Maya planted these crops together, as each plant helped the others to grow well. The tall corn plants provided a structure for the bean plants to climb up. The squash plants grew across the ground, stopping weeds from growing. The Maya also grew tomatoes, chilies, avocados, and cacao beans.

Corn, squash, and beans contain carbohydrates for energy as well as vitamins and minerals. These kept the Maya healthy.

Corn-u-copia

The Maya prepared corn in different ways to create a variety of dishes. First, the corn was soaked in a mixture made with ash or limestone. This made the corn more nutritious. Then, the corn was ground into a paste and pressed into flat tortillas, cooked inside corn husks, or made into a porridge.

This figurine shows a Maya woman preparing food. Her pet dog is at her side.

WOW!

The Maya used cacao beans as a type of **currency**, trading them for other food and resources. They also made them into a bitter drink that was served at religious rituals.

ASTRONOMY

The Maya were skilled astronomers who had an advanced knowledge and understanding of the night sky. Astronomy influenced many aspects of Maya life, from religion to city planning.

Looking up

The Maya didn't have telescopes, so all their observations were made with the naked eye. They kept records of what they saw and tracked the movement of the Sun, the Moon, the planets, and the stars. They used their records to accurately predict **eclipses** and **solstices**.

solar eclipse

The surviving Maya codices contain tables with predicted dates of solar and lunar eclipses. They also include the cycle of the planet Venus.

Observatories

Historians believe the Maya may have had observatories, such as El Caracol. At this site, a tall tower was built high above the trees to give astronomers a clear view of the skies above. Windows at the top of the tower were placed to align exactly with the path of Venus, so astronomers could move from window to window, following the movement of the planet.

El Caracol is located in the city of Chichén Itzá in Mexico.

Astronomy everywhere

The Maya used their knowledge of the movement of the Sun to create a calendar. They planned major events, such as battles, around the astrological calendar, waiting until changes in the movement of Venus to attack, as they believed this was the luckiest time. Religious celebrations were also timed to coincide with important astronomical events, such as solstices.

Many Maya buildings were built to interact with the path of the Sun and its light. At the spring and autumn **equinoxes**, the sunlight that hits El Castillo pyramid creates shadows that look like a snake sliding down the building.

TEST OF TIME

The remains of El Caracol look as if it once had a rounded dome on top, similar to modern observatories. Originally, El Caracol actually had a tall cylinder-shaped central tower, which has fallen apart over time. Today, observatories are built in high places with little **light pollution**, to give astronomers the best views.

curved snake shadow

THE MAYA CALENDAR

The Maya improved on calendars originally created by an earlier civilization to develop more sophisticated ways of keeping track of time. They used different systems for different purposes.

The sacred calendar

The Maya **sacred** calendar was 260 days long. There were two cycles within the calendar that happened at the same time—one cycle of 13 numbered days and one cycle of 20 named days. The combination of the two cycles gave each date in the calendar its own unique name, made up of a name and a number. The Maya believed certain dates were lucky or unlucky for performing certain tasks or actions, such as going to war.

This reconstruction of a Maya mural shows a priest taking part in a ceremony. Priests referred to the sacred calendar to choose lucky days for rituals.

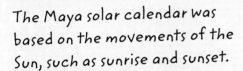

The Maya solar calendar was based on the movements of the Sun, such as sunrise and sunset.

The solar calendar

The Maya also followed a 365-day solar calendar. They divided this year into 18 months of 20 days, plus five days at the end of the year, which were considered unlucky. The solar and sacred calendars ran at the same time. It took 52 years for the calendars to return to their original starting places where the first days of both calendars happened at the same time.

The Long Count

The Maya used a third system called the Long Count to track dates over long periods of time. The Long Count was a continuous tracking of time from one date in the past. The Maya Long Count began on August 11, 3114 B.C.E. The Maya civilization did not exist at that time, but they believed that was the date Earth was created.

These glyphs represent the date February 11, 526 C.E., as part of the Long Count.

WOW!

During the unlucky five-day period at the end of the solar calendar, the Maya fasted and carried out sacrifices to please the gods and avoid bad luck.

THE MAYA BALL GAME

GENIUS ★ SPIRITUAL SPORT ★

Many civilizations in Mexico and Central America, including the Maya, played a similar ball game. This game wasn't just a sport for the Maya—it was an important religious ritual.

Aim of the game

The Maya ball game was played by two teams. The aim was to get a large rubber ball through a stone ring, similar to the game of basketball. However, players couldn't use their hands or feet. They had to hit the ball with their hips or other parts of the body.

(((BRAIN WAVE)))

The Maya made rubber for the balls from the sap of the rubber tree. They learned that mixing in sap from a vine made the rubber less brittle and more bouncy, which was perfect for balls!

This container is decorated with an image of a Maya ball player. He is wearing black body paint and thick padding to protect his body from the heavy rubber ball.

Religion and ritual

The Maya ball game had great religious significance and was a ritual connected to death and war. The game was also an important part of a Maya **myth** about two heroic twins. The Hero Twins were mythical twin brothers who eventually turned into the Sun and the Moon. Players may have taken part in the game to show their respect to the gods. Prisoners of war may have been sacrificed after the game as a religious offering.

Ball courts

The Maya built ball courts in the center of their cities, alongside important temples and royal homes. Each ball court had a long, thin central section with walls on either side. Stone hoops were built on the walls on both sides of the court.

Many Maya ball courts had sloping walls. The balls would bounce off the walls.

TEST OF TIME

A modern version of the ball game, called *ulama*, is still played today in a few areas of Mexico. *Ulama* is one of the oldest continuously played sports in the world.

The stone hoops in this ball court were decorated with glyphs.

ART

The Maya created finely crafted pieces of art from a variety of materials. Many of their artworks were made to be used in religious ceremonies.

GENIUS ★ RANGE OF MATERIALS ★

Creative carving

The Maya used carving to create many different types of art. Sculptors carved stelae, or huge statues of kings, from large chunks of stone. These statues were placed in and around important buildings in the center of cities. They also carved **intricate** details on buildings. Smaller carved figurines were made from jade and shells. These figurines were used in rituals and buried with important people.

The **hieroglyphic** stairway at Copán, Honduras, is decorated with over two thousand carved glyphs. They tell the history of royalty in the city. The stela is of a ruler of Copán.

Painted pottery

The Maya made a variety of ceramic objects, ranging from everyday pots to containers used in rituals. Religious ceramics were painted with colorful images of the gods and scenes from Maya myths, such as the story of the Hero Twins.

Some Maya ceramics were painted with intricate designs, such as this pot that shows the Hero Twins meeting the lords of the underworld.

Others have interesting shapes, such as this pot shaped like a crocodile.

Eccentric flints

One of the most highly skilled Maya crafts was making **eccentric** flints. Skilled craftspeople used stone tools to carve flint and obsidian into irregular shapes that represented animals, people, and gods. Eccentric flints are often found in tombs, so they probably had a religious meaning.

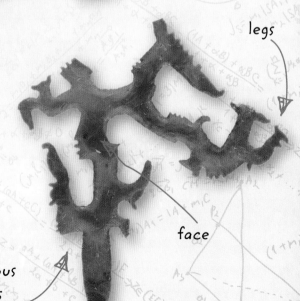

legs

face

This eccentric flint has various human shapes, including legs and the profile of a face.

CLOTHES

The clothes the Maya wore depended on social status. Ordinary people wore plain clothes, while wealthy merchants and powerful members of the elite wore jewelry and colorful clothing.

GENIUS ★ COLORFUL CLOTH

Spinning and weaving

To make cloth, Maya **weavers** began by spinning cotton and cactus fibers into thread. Then, they colored the threads using natural dyes, such as a red dye made from insects or a purple dye **extracted** from shells. They wove the threads into cloth on a **loom**. The top part of the loom was attached to a tree or a wall and the bottom part was tied around the weaver's waist.

TEST OF TIME

Today, the Maya are famous for their colorful **textiles**. Many are still woven by hand on the same type of loom that their **ancestors** used.

This modern Maya woman weaves using a traditional loom.

All about accessories

Rich and important Maya wore accessories as **status symbols**. Both men and women had pierced ears and they wore large earrings called earflares to stretch out the piercings. They also wore necklaces and bracelets made from shells and valuable stones. Maya rulers wore huge headdresses made from colorful feathers.

Shaping jade into jewelry, such as these earflares and this necklace, was a slow and difficult process. Jade is a very hard stone. It took a long time for craftspeople to shape and polish it with the tools they had available.

The earrings, bracelets, and necklace on this statue of a Maya woman, found in Mexico, suggest she was part of the elite.

29

GLOSSARY

ancestor A family member who lived long ago

architecture The practice of designing and constructing buildings

astronomy The study of space, stars, and planets

city-state A city and the area around it that function as an independent country

civilization The stage of a human society, such as its culture and way of life

codices Handwritten books

culture The beliefs and customs of a group of people

currency The system of money in a particular country

diverse Showing variety

eccentric Unusual or strange

eclipse When a planet passes through the shadow of another planet

elite The richest or most powerful people in society

equinox One of two occasions in the year when day and night are the same length

extract The juice or liquid removed from a plant

fertile Describes soil in which plants grow well

flint A hard type of rock that can be chipped and shaped into sharp objects

glyph A symbol that represents a word or a sound

hastily Done quickly without time to plan

heir A person entitled to property or rank after a death

hierarchy A system in which people or things are organized according to their importance

hieroglyphics The ancient Egyptian system of picture writing

import To receive goods for sale from a foreign area

intricate Very complicated or highly detailed

irrigation The process of bringing water to farmland in order to grow crops

landscape The visible features of a land

light pollution Human-made lights shining at night, disrupting natural cycles and blocking the view of stars

loom A machine used to weave thread into fabric

myth An invented story related to history

natural resources Materials or substances from nature that can be used to earn money

noble To have a high rank or title

plaster A material that becomes hard as it dries

plaza An open public area in a town or city

rain forest A tropical forest in an area with high rainfall

regent A person who rules in place of a king or queen who is either too young or too sick to rule

ritual A religious ceremony in which actions are performed in a particular order

sacred Of deep religious importance

sacrifice When a living thing is killed to please the gods

scribe A person who writes documents by hand

solstice The days in which the Sun is at its northernmost or southernmost points

status symbol An object that people use or display to show how important or rich they are

symbolize To represent something though the use of an object

textile A type of cloth or woven fabric

thatched Describes something built using straw or dried plants

weaver A person who creates fabrics by crossing threads together

TIMELINE

3114 B.C.E.	The world is created, according to the Maya Long Count calendar.
1500 B.C.E.	The first Maya settle in small villages in Central America and Mexico.
200 C.E.	The first Maya cities are built.
250 to 900	Maya civilization is at its height during the Classic Period.
615 to 683	Pakal the Great rules over the city of Palenque.
900	Southern Maya cities begin to decline.
1500s	Spanish invaders destroy most of the Maya civilization.

INDEX

LEARNING MORE

Websites

www.pbs.org/wgbh/nova/ancient/map-of-the-maya-world.html

http://maya.nmai.si.edu/calendar

www.dkfindout.com/us/history/mayans/

Books

Honders, Christine. *Ancient Maya Culture.* PowerKids Press, 2016.

Spilsbury, Louise. *Forensic Investigations of the Maya.* Crabtree Publishing, 2019.

Stuckey, Rachel. *Ancient Maya Inside Out.* Crabtree Publishing, 2017.